HUMAN BODY SYSTEMS

The Human
Digestive System

By Cassie M. Lawton

Cavendish
Square

New York

Published in 2021 by Cavendish Square Publishing, LLC
243 5th Avenue, Suite 136, New York, NY 10016

First Edition

Website: cavendishsq.com

This publication represents the opinions and views of the author based on his or her personal experience, knowledge, and research. The information in this book serves as a general guide only. The author and publisher have used their best efforts in preparing this book and disclaim liability rising directly or indirectly from the use and application of this book.

Portions of this work were originally authored by John M. Shea, MD, and published as *The Digestive System (The Human Body)*. All new material this edition authored by Cassie M. Lawton.

All websites were available and accurate when this book was sent to press.

Library of Congress Cataloging-in-Publication Data

Names: Lawton, Cassie M., author.
Title: The human digestive system / Cassie M. Lawton.
Description: First edition. | New York, NY : Cavendish Square Publishing, 2021. |
Series: The inside guide: human body systems | Includes index.
Identifiers: LCCN 2019051921 (print) | LCCN 2019051922 (ebook) |
ISBN 9781502657237 (library binding) | ISBN 9781502657213 (paperback) |
ISBN 9781502657220 (set) | ISBN 9781502657244 (ebook)
Subjects: LCSH: Digestive organs–Juvenile literature.
Classification: LCC QP145 .L39 2021 (print) | LCC QP145 (ebook) |
DDC 612.3–dc23
LC record available at https://lccn.loc.gov/2019051921
LC ebook record available at https://lccn.loc.gov/2019051922

Editor: Kristen Susienka
Copy Editor: Nathan Heidelberger
Designer: Deanna Paternostro

The photographs in this book are used by permission and through the courtesy of: Cover Sebastian Kaulitzki/Shutterstock.com; p. 4 ASDF_MEDIA/Shutterstock.com; p. 6 La Gorda/Shutterstock.com; p. 7 bitt24/Shutterstock.com; p. 8 Gaus Alex/Shutterstock.com; p. 9 (top) Kiian Oksana/Shutterstock.com; p. 9 (bottom) Anton Starikov/Shutterstock.com; p. 10 noPPonPat/Shutterstock.com; p. 11 Andrey_Popov/Shutterstock.com; p. 13 VAZZEN/Shutterstock.com; p. 14 Crevis/Shutterstock.com; p. 15 Rost9/Shutterstock.com; p. 16 Vecton/Shutterstock.com; p. 18 Nerthuz/Shutterstock.com; pp. 18-19 Kateryna Kon/Shutterstock.com; p. 19 Life science/Shutterstock.com; p. 21 wavebreakmedia/Shutterstock.com; p. 22 fizkes/Shutterstock.com; p. 24 Lightspring/Shutterstock.com; pp. 24-25 Tyler Olson/Shutterstock.com; p. 25 Alena Veasey/Shutterstock.com; p. 27 (top) Aleksei Potov/Shutterstock.com; p. 27 (bottom) gst/Shutterstock.com; p. 28 (top) Monkey Business Images/Shutterstock.com; p. 28 (bottom) beats1/Shutterstock.com; p. 29 (top left) ESB Professional/Shutterstock.com; p. 29 (top right) nd3000/Shutterstock.com; p. 29 (bottom) vectorfusionart/Shutterstock.com.

Some of the images in this book illustrate individuals who are models. The depictions do not imply actual situations or events.

CPSIA compliance information: Batch #CS20CSQ: For further information contact Cavendish Square Publishing LLC, New York, New York, at 1-877-980-4450.

Printed in the United States of America

Find us on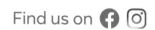

CONTENTS

Food helps people live. Everyone needs to eat!

EATING TO LIVE

Food is an important part of life. All living things need it to survive. More specifically, they need nutrients. Nutrients are substances found in food that provide energy and materials the body needs to grow. Some living things, such as plants, make their own food from sunlight. This process is called photosynthesis. Other **organisms**, such as extremely small **bacteria**, need only a tiny amount of nutrients to grow.

The human body, however, has many parts. It needs a lot of nutrients to keep working. If they have to, humans can survive more than a week without food or a couple of days without water, but without enough nutrients, the human body doesn't work properly. The food we eat and drink—whether it's an apple, a slice of pizza, or a glass of milk—contains nutrients our body needs. Our bodies must first break these foods down into very small pieces so we can use the nutrients in them. The process of breaking down food into basic nutrients is called digestion. It allows the body to get nutrients it needs and get rid of other materials it doesn't need. Digestion takes place in the body parts that make up the digestive system.

Fast Fact
Doctors recommend people drink about 8 cups (2 liters) of water every day.

Breaking Down the Digestive System

Think of the digestive system as one continuous tract, or tube. It starts with the mouth, where we put food and drinks in, and ends with the anus, where undigested material, called waste, leaves the body. Every part of the digestive system has a specific job to help us get the most nutrients from our food. Most jobs involve breaking down food and moving nutrients from the digestive tract to the bloodstream. From there, blood carries the nutrients to the parts of the body that need them.

The Joy of Food

Nutrients in our food play a special part in our health. Carbohydrates, which include sugars and **starches**, are the body's main source of energy. Proteins—which are made up of chemicals called amino acids—are the basic building blocks for the human body. Lipids, sometimes known as fats, are made from chemicals called fatty acids. They're important for both growth and energy. However, too much fat can lead to dangerous problems such as heart attacks.

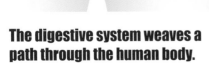

The digestive system weaves a path through the human body.

VITAMINS AND MINERALS

Vitamins and minerals are important parts of food. They help the body function. There are many kinds of vitamins and minerals, and each plays a very special part in our health. For example, vitamin A is used by the eyes to help with vision. An example of a food with vitamin A is a carrot. Vitamin C is used by the **immune system** to help fight off illnesses and to heal cuts. You can get vitamin C from orange juice, strawberries, and kale. Minerals are natural substances such as calcium and zinc. The human body needs these substances to carry out many processes, including the growth of bones.

Eating a balanced diet can help people make sure their digestive system is taking in all the nutrients they need.

Salmon is a source of a healthy fat called omega-3.

Where Are Those Nutrients?

Vitamins	Where Do We Find Them?
A	carrots, leafy vegetables, butter, fish oil
B1, B2, B3, B6	whole grains, nuts, many vegetables
B12	fish, meat, dairy, chicken, eggs
C	citrus fruit (lemons, oranges), tomatoes
D	fish, fortified milk, yogurt, eggs
E	vegetables, nuts
K	leafy vegetables (lettuce, spinach, kale)

Minerals	Where Do We Find Them?
calcium	dairy products, leafy vegetables, grains
iron	meat, nuts, eggs, leafy vegetables, beans, fish
potassium	bananas, beans, nuts, fish
sodium	meat, vegetables, bread
zinc	fish, beans, eggs, meat, nuts

People need to eat plenty of carbohydrates, proteins, and fiber, and drink enough water to stay healthy.

Water is extremely important for the body. More than half the human body is made of water, and we need to drink enough every day to help keep our bodies well **hydrated**. If someone doesn't get enough water, they could end up in the hospital. On the other hand, too much water can hurt a person too.

Fiber is a substance that helps regulate the digestive system, or keep it running properly. Our bodies don't digest and absorb, or take in, fiber for growth and health. Instead, undigested fiber helps push food forward through the digestive tract.

Fast Fact

Some foods that have lots of fiber are oatmeal, baked beans, and boiled broccoli.

Staying hydrated will help your digestive system work well!

9

People use their teeth to grind their food before it enters the rest of the digestive system.

DIGESTION IN ACTION

Each part of the digestive system has its own part to play in helping the human body function. As food moves along the digestive tract, it goes through many stages.

Eating

The first step in transforming food into nutrients begins in the mouth. Teeth bite and grind food into smaller, softer pieces. The mouth produces saliva, or spit, which makes food easier to chew and swallow. Saliva also contains chemicals known as **enzymes**. Enzymes begin to break food down into nutrients small enough for the body to absorb.

Once the food is small and soft enough, it's ready to be swallowed. The tongue pushes the food toward the back of the throat and down a muscular tube, called the esophagus, that connects the

Fast Fact

The human tongue is covered with tiny bumps called "taste buds" that recognize foods that taste sweet, salty, sour, bitter, and umami. Umami is a savory flavor that can be found in foods like meat, mushrooms, and cheese.

Taste buds are tiny bumps on the top of your tongue.

11

mouth to the stomach. When the muscles of the esophagus become stretched with food, they squeeze and push the food down in a process called peristalsis.

Strong Stomachs

From the esophagus, food empties into the stomach. This is a muscular sac about the size of your fist, but it can expand to hold a large meal. The stomach contains an extremely strong acid that helps **dissolve** food while also killing many types of bacteria. The stomach also produces an enzyme called pepsin that breaks down proteins into smaller substances called peptides and amino acids.

The stomach can hold food from your last meal for hours. It slowly releases partially digested food into the next part of the digestive system—the small intestine—a little at a time. Any food that's too big for the small intestine stays in the stomach longer, where the acid and pepsin continue to break it down further.

The Small Intestine

The small intestine is where most of the digestion and absorption of nutrients takes place. Food coming from the stomach mixes with enzymes and fluids coming from the **pancreas**. The fluids **neutralize** the stomach acids, while the enzymes finish breaking down the food into the basic building blocks of nutrition, like amino acids, vitamins, and minerals.

On the inside wall of the small intestine are thousands of very tiny, finger-like folds called villi. The villi have special channels, or tunnels, that allow the nutrients to leave the small intestine and enter the bloodstream. When the food we eat exits the small intestine, there's nothing left

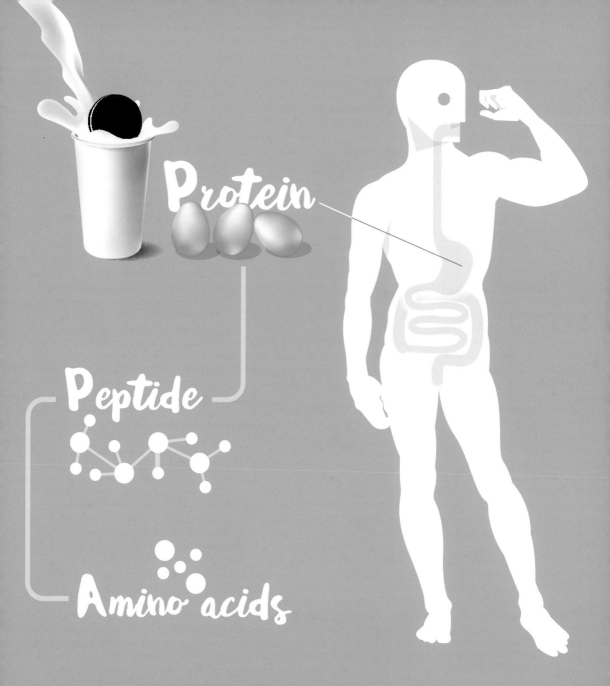

Protein

Peptide

Amino acids

Proteins are broken down into peptides and amino acids during digestion.

SORES OF THE STOMACH AND SMALL INTESTINE

Peptic ulcers are small wounds in the stomach, small intestine, and esophagus walls that can be extremely painful. They develop over time and can cause someone so much pain that they need surgery. Peptic ulcers usually develop when bacteria or another substance eats away at the lining of the wall, which is coated with a substance called mucus. When the mucus lining is reduced in size, it can't protect against digestive acids, like it's meant to. Instead, the acids are able to hurt the walls of the digestive system, causing ulcer sores to form.

For many years, doctors thought ulcers were caused by stress and too much stomach acid. Recently, scientists have discovered that a bacterium called *Helicobacter pylori* is the most common cause of the wounds. Drugs that kill bacteria, called antibiotics, have helped cure many people of this painful condition.

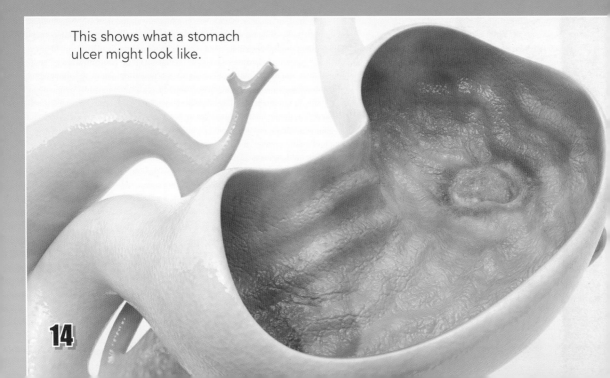

This shows what a stomach ulcer might look like.

but water, some minerals, and material we can't digest, such as fiber. This material eventually gets moved through the other players in digestion and out of the human body as waste.

This illustration imagines what villi look like inside the small intestine.

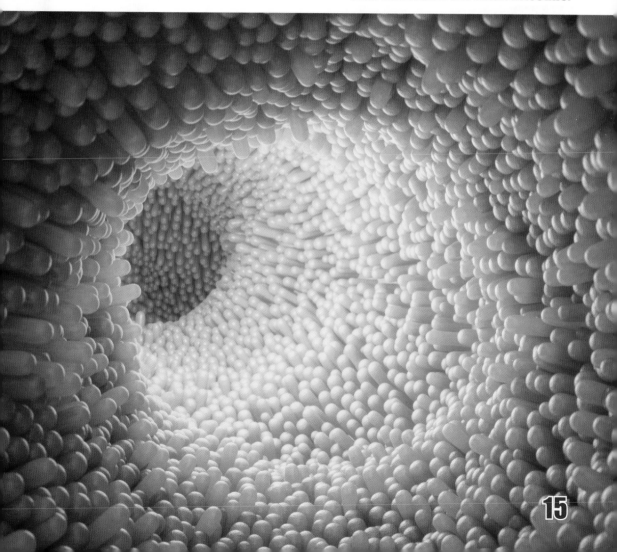

This diagram shows the different parts involved in the digestive system.

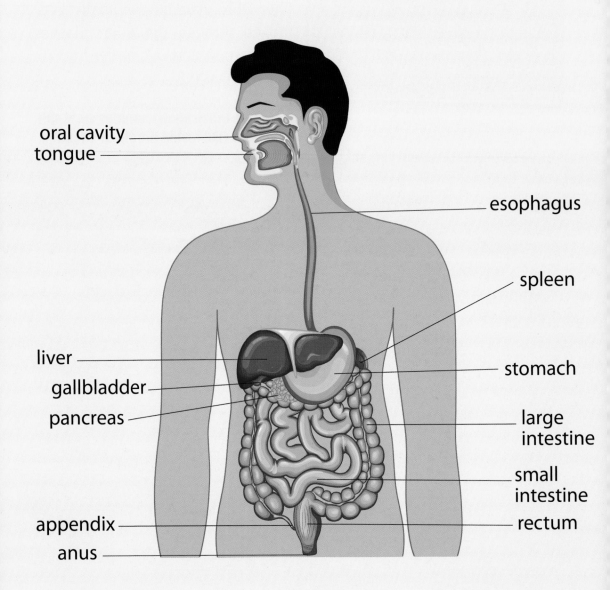

oral cavity
tongue
esophagus
spleen
liver
gallbladder
pancreas
stomach
large intestine
small intestine
appendix
anus
rectum

Chapter Three

THE END OF DIGESTION

Playing a part in digestion are many more organs inside the human body. They all work together to complete the digestion process.

The Pancreas

While most digestion occurs in the small intestine, many enzymes that aid digestion are made in the pancreas. The pancreas releases pancreatic juices, which contain hundreds of different enzymes. Each of these breaks down a specific nutrient into its basic building blocks. Pancreatic juices also help neutralize acids from the stomach. Outside of digestion, the pancreas is also important for producing insulin, a hormone that helps control sugar levels in our blood.

Supporting Players

While it isn't connected directly to the digestive tract, the liver plays an important role in digestion too. When nutrients are absorbed into the blood by the small intestine, they're first carried to the liver. The liver stores some of these nutrients for future use. It also protects the body by cleaning the

Fast Fact

Despite its name, the "small" intestine is, in fact, the longest part in the human body—it's over 20 feet (6 meters) long!

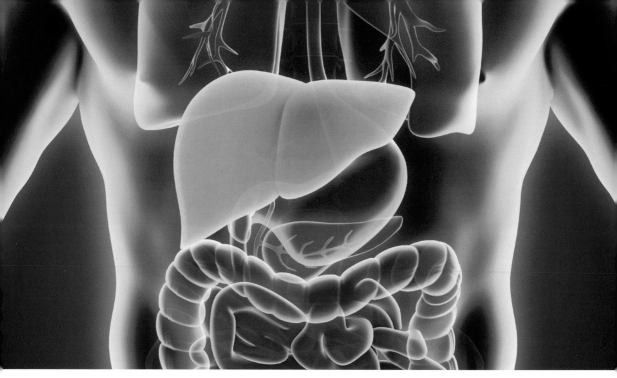

The liver plays supporting parts in the main digestion process.

blood of harmful substances that may have been accidentally absorbed by the small intestine.

The gallbladder is a small, muscular sac that sits right underneath the liver. Unlike its neighbor, the gallbladder is directly involved with human digestion. Its job is to store a special fluid called bile, which is a green liquid made in the liver. Bile contains special salts that help digest fats.

Fast Fact

The bile salts in the gallbladder usually stay dissolved in the bile, but sometimes they crystallize, or harden, to form a tough material called a gallstone. Eating meals that are low in fat can help prevent the pain caused by gallstones. However, sometimes surgery is necessary to remove the stones.

When you eat a fatty meal, the gallbladder releases a small amount of bile into the small intestine to help dissolve and break down the fat.

Digestion Ends

Most of our food's nutrients are digested and absorbed in the small intestine. The main job of the colon—the longest section of the large intestine—is to absorb water and minerals. About 8 cups (1.9 L) of watery material enter the colon daily, and about 7 cups (1.7 L) of water are absorbed into the blood. What's left is called feces, which is undigested food and bacteria. Other names for feces are poop and waste.

Waste travels through the colon the same way food travels down the esophagus and through the small intestine—by peristalsis. Normally, waste travels through the colon slowly, allowing the body time to absorb water. When we eat a meal, however, our brain signals the colon to speed up the transfer of waste.

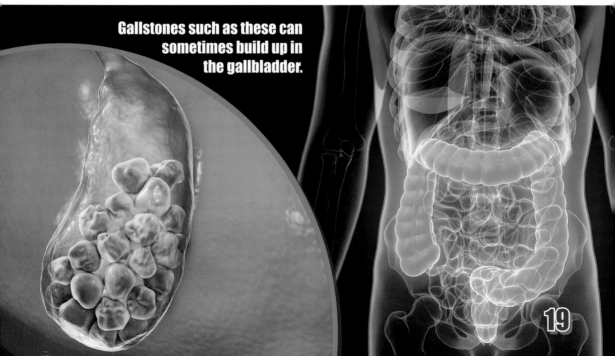

The large intestine helps in the body's waste removal process.

Gallstones such as these can sometimes build up in the gallbladder.

19

The Final Act

You might not believe it, but there are more bacteria in your body than there are human cells! Most of that bacteria can be found in your colon. These bacteria eat undigested food in your colon and are mostly helpful. They help crowd out bacteria that can make you sick. Some make vitamin K that your body can use. Living and dead bacteria make up about half of human feces! The other half is undigested food.

After water is absorbed from the undigested food waste, the colon pushes the remaining materials—feces (or poop)—into the rectum. The rectum acts as a storage area until there's an appropriate time to eliminate the feces. This is a process known as defecation, pooping, or having a bowel movement. Together, the small intestine and large intestine are known as the bowel. This is where the phrase "bowel movement" comes from.

Defecation is the passage of feces through the anus, which is the opening through which waste is released from the rectum. Defecation is controlled by muscular rings known as sphincters. When the sphincters relax, it allows the feces to pass from the body. You may find yourself holding your breath and pushing with the muscles near your stomach when you're having a bowel movement. This increases pressure in the **abdomen**, or stomach region of the body, and helps push the feces out of the body. It might be a bit gross, but it's an important part of the digestion process—and every living thing has to get rid of waste somehow!

WHAT'S CONSTIPATION?

When we don't have a bowel movement as often as we normally do, waste stays in the large intestine longer, and more water is absorbed into the body. This makes the feces harder than normal and can make defecation painful. This is called constipation. Everyone experiences constipation at some point, but it can be prevented! Drink plenty of water, eat plenty of vegetables, and exercise. Doing activities such as running, swimming, or other exercises can make feces travel through the colon faster and more easily. It's important to always keep your body healthy, and having regular bowel movements is part of that process.

Staying active helps your digestive system stay healthy and prevents the body from getting constipated.

Sometimes, food can cause an upset stomach or sick feeling.

TAKING CARE OF YOUR BODY

By eating food and drinking water, we can keep our bodies working well. However, we also risk letting harmful bacteria into our bodies. Eating or drinking too much of something can also lead to diseases and disorders.

Problems From Food and Water

The acid in your stomach helps kill most bacteria. However, some bacteria are very **hardy** and aren't hurt by stomach acid. They can give us food poisoning, which can cause vomiting—throwing up—and stomach pain. These bacteria can live in undercooked meat, spoiled dairy products, and unwashed vegetables. Washing and cooking food properly and making sure it's stored in the refrigerator are two ways to help prevent food poisoning.

People can also get sick when they drink water that contains germs. These germs often stop the absorption of water in the colon, resulting in feces mixed with large amounts of water, which is known as diarrhea. This can cause the body to lose a lot of water, and a lack of water is harmful to important organs such as the kidneys and the brain.

Appendicitis

A condition called appendicitis can cause abdominal pain. Appendicitis is an **infection** of a small body part called the appendix, which is located where the small and large intestines meet. The actual purpose of the appendix is unknown, which is actually a good thing for humans. It can be taken out of the human body without causing problems for other parts!

The appendix is a pouch about the size of your pinky finger. On very rare occasions, this pouch can get blocked by feces and bacteria. The bacteria continue to grow in the appendix. Since the opening to the pouch is blocked, the appendix begins to stretch, like a balloon. This causes very sharp and severe pain in the abdomen.

If the appendix continues to stretch, it will eventually rupture, or burst. This will spread bacteria throughout the body, making the patient very sick very quickly. In some cases, the person could die. Surgeons must remove the appendix to stop the infection.

Other Problems

There are many other causes of abdominal pain, and most don't need surgery. Hospitals have special machines that use a method called computed tomography, or CT, to scan the body for problems. These machines take hundreds of X-rays very quickly and put them together on a computer, which allows doctors to see inside the abdomen. Many doctors also use **ultrasound** machines to see images of a patient's abdomen right at their bedside.

If you're having stomach pains, a
CT scan can help determine why.

Allergies

Some people experience very serious allergic reactions when they eat certain foods, such as peanuts or strawberries. The immune system thinks the food is a germ, so it releases chemicals to help fight the "infection." These chemicals can do incredible damage to the body. They can cause swelling around the windpipe, making it difficult for the person to breathe. People with food allergies must avoid even the tiniest piece of the food they're allergic to. Some people don't even have to eat the food—they can have an allergic reaction if food is being cooked or eaten nearby. People can manage their food allergies by avoiding contact with the food. For severe cases, people can use a special device with a chemical called epinephrine inside that can save someone's life if they're experiencing a bad allergic reaction.

Taking Charge of Your Health

Fiber is an extremely important part of our diet, even though it doesn't supply any vitamins or minerals. Rather, fiber remains undigested as it travels though the digestive system.

Fast Fact

Common food allergies include allergies to peanuts, wheat, milk, fish, shellfish, soybeans, and tree nuts.

Food allergies can be very serious. It's important to always check labels carefully if you have a food allergy.

FOOD ALLERGIES and INTOLERANCES

Please speak to our staff about the ingredients in your meal, when making your order.

Thank you.

FOOD INTOLERANCE

Sometimes the problems we have with our digestive systems are due to the foods we eat. Lactose is a type of carbohydrate found in dairy products. For most people, lactose is broken down by enzymes found in the small intestine. However, one out of every six Americans is lactose intolerant. That means they can't digest lactose. This can result in abdominal pain, cramping, **nausea**, and diarrhea.

Gluten is a protein found in many types of flours, including wheat and rye. If someone has celiac disease, their immune system thinks gluten is a germ and tries to attack the protein. Unfortunately, the immune system does a lot of damage to the digestive system during these attacks, which can cause abdominal pain, diarrhea, and bloating. These attacks can be prevented by avoiding foods that contain gluten. Many restaurants and grocery stores now have gluten-free options and aisles to help people avoid gluten, either out of need or by choice.

It provides the small and large intestines with something to push against during peristalsis. Without fiber in the colon, peristalsis slows down and can even stop. This can lead to constipation.

Scientists also believe a diet rich in fiber helps prevent diseases such as **diabetes** and heart disease. Fiber can be found in most foods that come from plants, including vegetables, fruits, and whole wheat bread.

You can help maintain good digestive health by eating a wide variety of foods. Packaged and junk foods may taste good, but they're often loaded with fat and sugar. Without other nutrients, such as protein and vitamins, to balance this, the excess fat is stored throughout the

Fast Fact

Fiber helps you feel full. It also helps prevent the absorption of fat in the small intestine.

Eating healthy foods is good for your digestive system and your body's other systems too!

body. This can lead to a condition called obesity, which means weighing far more than you should for your height. It can also cause future medical problems, including diabetes, heart disease, **stroke**, and **cancer**.

A good way to track the nutrients in your food is by using nutrition labels. Many such labels break down a food or meal's makeup. They can be found on most foods you can buy.

Taking care of your body begins by carefully choosing what you put inside it, so make sure what you're eating and drinking helps you rather than harms you.

Nutrition Facts		
Serving Size 100 g		
Amount Per Serving		
Calories 250	Calories from fat 10	
	% Daily Value*	
Total Fat 4%		4%
Saturated Fat 1.5%		4%
Trans Fat		
Cholesterol 50mg		28%
Sodium 150mg		15%
Total Carbohydrate 10g		3%
Dietary Fiber 5g		
Sugars 3g		
Protein 16%		
Vitamin A 1%	**Vitamin C** 3%	
Calcium 2%	**Iron** 2%	

*Percent Daily Values are based on a 2,000 calorie diet. Your daily values may be higher or lower depending on your calorie needs.

THINK ABOUT IT!

1. How can you make sure to get enough nutrients during a day?

2. Name a few foods that are rich in vitamins and minerals.

3. Why is water so important? Think about how much water you drink every day. Do you get enough? How can you make sure to stay hydrated?

4. What are some ways you can keep your digestive system healthy?

5. How can you prevent diseases related to digestion?

GLOSSARY

abdomen: The part of the body between the chest and hips.

bacteria: Tiny creatures that can only be seen with a microscope.

cancer: A disease caused by the uncontrolled growth of cells in the body.

diabetes: A disorder that causes the body to produce excess urine and causes high levels of sugar in the blood.

dissolve: To break down something solid by mixing it with a liquid.

enzyme: A protein made in the body that helps chemical reactions occur.

hardy: Strong.

hydrated: Having a healthy amount of water in the body.

immune system: The parts of the body that fight germs and keep it healthy.

infection: The spread of germs inside the body, causing illness.

nausea: An unsettled feeling in the stomach, or feeling like you will throw up.

neutralize: To make something ineffective and remove its ability to cause harm.

organism: A living creature.

pancreas: A part of the body that produces enzymes and hormones.

savory: A rich, meaty flavor.

starch: A carbohydrate made by and stored in plants.

stroke: A sudden blockage or break of a blood vessel in the brain.

ultrasound: A method for seeing internal body parts using sound waves that people cannot hear.

Books

Gomdori Co. and Hyun-Dong Han. *Survive! The Human Body Vol. 1: The Digestive System*. San Francisco, CA: No Starch Press, 2013.

Johnson, Rebecca L. *Your Digestive System*. Minneapolis, MN: Lerner Publishing Group, 2013.

Woolf, Alex. *You Wouldn't Want to Live Without Poop!* London, UK: Franklin Watts, 2016.

Websites

DK Find Out: Digestion

www.dkfindout.com/us/human-body/digestion
This interactive website from DK Find Out explores the digestive system in detail.

Nat Geo Kids: Human Digestive System

www.natgeokids.com/uk/discover/science/general-science/your-digestive-system
This website is full of detailed illustrations that help make learning about the digestive system fun.

Your Digestive System

kidshealth.org/en/kids/digestive-system.html
Learn about the digestive system by following what happens to pizza and orange slices once they enter your mouth.

INDEX